The Bonds of Sisterhood

A Guide to Building Your Tribe

Norine C. Fahie

Contents

Dedication

To Mommy,

Your love has been the source of my strength, and your teachings are the foundation of my wisdom. Although our relationship wasn't always perfect, those challenges helped me learn the most profound lessons on connection, resilience, and the beauty of sisterhood. By your example, I learned how to bond with other women, share their joys, support them through tough times, and stand together in loyal solidarity.

Your spirit will live on in every page of this book, every story of empowerment, and every celebration of sisterhood. Thank you for being my first sister, guiding light, and my inspiration. This book is for you and all the women who, like you, teach us the true meaning of love and mental fortitude. I miss you every day, Mommy. I love you with all my heart.

Norine

Acknowledgments

*T*hank you for all you've done to help me on this very personal journey.

First, I would like to thank my heavenly Father for his grace, love, and mercy. Your divine guidance has taught me that I am nothing without you, but I can accomplish everything with you. You are my salvation, and I live to serve only you.

To my husband, Ivan, you are my biggest supporter, soul mate, prayer partner, and best friend. You are God's gift to me and everyone you touch with your presence and your wonderful words of wisdom. You came into my life as my answered prayer after a long emotional discussion with my heavenly Father. Our love embodies genuine love and commitment toward each other and denotes a strong foundation for our marriage. Being married to you has taught me what true patience and partnership look like and what it feels like to have someone who cares about my happiness. Because of your love and support, I can confidently walk in my power and be the woman God has called me to be. To date, we have overcome some challenges, exceeded our expectations, and proved that anything is possible when we stay united with our intentions and grounded in God's word.

To my children and grandchildren, the fruits of my womb… my air. You are my greatest blessings and the joys of my life. You have inspired me to become the mother you needed in every situation and have held me accountable in the moments when I fell short. You are extensions of me, and the proof that my life serves a greater purpose. Each of you is a beautiful puzzle piece in the bigger picture of my life, and I am fortunate and grateful to have you.

To my friends, thank you for your blind support of me. I appreciate your encouragement and belief in my vision. You are a loyal tribe, and I thank God for placing you in my life at the right moments. Your encouragement has been a true blessing and the motivation I needed to keep going.

Preface

Sisterhood is a powerful and multifaceted concept that encompasses the bonds we share, the support we give, and the unity we create among women. It is a source of immense strength, joy, and personal growth. This book was written to delve into the various aspects of sisterhood, exploring its benefits, joys, and profound importance in our lives.

Throughout this book, I aim to provide women with valuable tools to recognize and cultivate true sisterhood. We will explore what to look for in these relationships, how to nurture them, and how they can be a source of empowerment and resilience. Additionally, we will consider the future of sisterhood, envisioning how these bonds can continue to evolve and strengthen in our ever-changing world.

As I started this journey of writing about sisterhood, I drew deeply from my personal experiences and stories. My relationships with the incredible women in my life have shaped my understanding of what sisterhood truly means. Through the highs and lows, the laughter and the tears, I have learned invaluable lessons that I am eager to share with you.

Each chapter begins with an encouraging quote from a remarkable woman that aligns with the chapter's topic. Drawing on the wisdom of women who have experienced and understood the power of sisterhood, these quotes offer a significant reminder of the strength we can find in each other.

Additionally, I have compiled these personal narratives with valuable information about sisterhood. My goal is to create a rich tapestry of insights that are both relatable and informative. By sharing my journey, I hope to inspire you to reflect on your experiences and recognize the sisterhoods that have played a significant role in your life.

At the end of each chapter, you will find two reflective questions. These questions are intended to encourage deeper thought and personal reflection on the chapter's topic. By engaging with these questions, you will be able to connect more intimately with the material and apply the lessons to your own life.

This book is a celebration of sisterhood in all its forms. It is an invitation to explore, cherish, and invest in the relationships that lift us up and make us stronger. I hope that as you read, you will find inspiration, encouragement, and practical guidance to enhance your own sisterhoods and build new ones that will enrich your life.

Thank you for embarking on this journey with me. Together, let us honor the bonds of sisterhood and embrace the transformative power they hold.

Peace and Blessings,
Norine C. Fahie

"*Sisterhood means if you happen to be in Burma and I happen to be in San Diego and I'm married to someone who is very jealous and you're married to somebody who is very possessive, if you call me in the middle of the night, I have to come.*"

~Maya Angelou

Sisterhood

*B*efore I knew what the term sisterhood meant, I thought it meant sisters in the hood… don't judge me! Then I thought to myself, well, that couldn't be me because I've never lived in the hood. Growing up with four sisters, you would think I would be an expert on sisterhood, but I'm not. Our life was so tumultuous that I don't think we had a chance to get our sisterhood on. We lived in a house where there was a lot of domestic abuse, physically and emotionally. It was crazy! All we ever did was go to school, and when we were at home, we would play school. Going to church was intermittent, but watching church on TV was a convenient weekly affair! Oh, and chores! Chile, island parents didn't play when it came to chores! They can find the smallest thing and make a chore out of it. We were constantly doing something! So, maybe they didn't know how to build a sisterhood because no one ever taught them how.

But what is sisterhood, really? It's more than just sharing DNA or growing up under the same roof. Sisterhood is a bond of trust, support, and love between women, whether they are related by blood or connected by shared experiences and values. It's about lifting each other up, holding space for one another, and creating a safe environment where we can be vulnerable without fear of judgment. And for me, having three older sisters should've meant more of that, but it didn't.

In those rare moments when I had time for myself, I spent a lot of time daydreaming. I was at the age when girls played with dolls and created their alternate realities of how motherhood and family life were going to be when they grew up. Well…we were not allowed to play with dolls for fear it would encourage us to get pregnant! Crazy, right? Anyhoo, I had to get creative. This is gonna sound weird, but I used to have some little silver scissors that I would make into dolls. Remember those? We used them in elementary school. Not the ones with pointy tips. The ones with rounded edges. I used to bend them back so that the part that cut became the legs, and the circle parts you put your fingers through became the head. Then I would find little pieces of cardboard for the arms and scraps from whatever fabric Mom was using, to make beautiful creations and dress them up. They were my sisters. I used to tell them everything! I never named them, but they were my best friends. My first tribe!

Fast forward to my moving to Illinois, where I have no family, no friends, and no support system. Yes, there was a man in the picture…mind your business! However, it was so much more than that. Moving from the Virgin Islands to America with two toddlers was a promise of a better life for myself and my children. The man was just the vehicle that got me here. Everyone speaks of the American Dream, but what is it really? I felt very alone and out of place here in a country I knew nothing about! When you're used to greeting people and being greeted with Good Morning, Good Afternoon, and Good Evening, and you move to an area where a head nod is a greeting, it confuses and humbles you at the same time. A head nod! What does that mean? Don't even get me started on children answering their parents by saying "what" and telling them they're going somewhere as opposed to asking permission to go. Our culture is built on respect, and we wouldn't dare speak to our parents that way, but chile, that is a story for another book! Not only do I have to get used to four seasons of weather and get acclimated with the African American experience, but now I must learn a new way of communicating because no one cared about my cultural norms! I was in Rome, and the women were different! They didn't move the way I moved. They didn't speak the way I spoke, and they didn't treat women the way I treated women. Some looked me up and down, rolled their eyes, and walked away. Others made fun of me because I had a heavy dialect, and I was told to "speak English!" Um, RUDE! I may have been speaking Creole or broken English, but it was English! This just solidified for me how hard my journey would be to become friendly with the women here. So, I kept to myself and observed them from afar.

I asked myself, why do I need the friendship of women anyway? If they're going to be funny acting, I could do without them, that's for sure. I concluded that we need each other for many reasons. First and foremost, our friendships provide a sense of emotional support and understanding that is often difficult to find elsewhere. We can relate to each other's experiences in such a unique way, sharing common challenges and joys that are specific to the female experience. This creates a bond of empathy and understanding between us that can be invaluable when taking on the ebbs and flows of life. Our friendships also offer a safe space for vulnerability and sharing, where we can express our thoughts and feelings without fear of judgment or shame. This emotional support can help us navigate difficult times and build resilience.

In addition to emotional support, our friendships offer opportunities for personal growth and learning. We can learn from each other's experiences and perspectives, gaining insights we may not have considered otherwise. Our networks can also offer professional support, providing opportunities for mentorship and collaboration that can help us advance in our careers. These friendships can also foster a sense of community and belonging, connecting us to a larger network of people who share similar values and interests. So…like it or not, we need each other to support, inspire, and challenge ourselves personally and professionally. Period!

How do you empower the women around you?

_____

_____

_____

_____

_____

_____

_____

_____

_____

_____

_____

_____

_____

_____

_____

_____

The Bonds Of Sisterhood

What have you done to make your sisterhood more inclusive?

_____

_____

_____

_____

_____

_____

_____

_____

_____

_____

_____

_____

_____

_____

_____

_____

_____

"Surround yourself with people who add value to your life. Who challenge you to be greater than you were yesterday. Who sprinkle magic into your existence, just like you do to theirs. Life isn't meant to be done alone. Find your tribe, and journey freely and loyally together."

~Alex Elle

Your Vibe Determines Your Tribe

There's an adage that states, "Beware of the company you keep." Even the Bible speaks of this in 1 Corinthians 15:33 (NIV), which states, "Bad company corrupts good character." No one wants to be judged by the company they keep, so you must be vigilant in your vetting process. Here I am in America, surrounded by women who didn't make me feel welcome and whom I couldn't trust. I couldn't fathom why they didn't feel like I could fit in with their clique! Was it the way I dressed? Was it because I was reserved? Was it because I had an accent? Was it because I was skinny? Was it me? NO! It was them! It was their insecurities. It was what they thought made me different from them. It was their…dare I say…jealousy? That's not my word, but I've been told that's what was going on, and I couldn't come up with another explanation. I've never been part of the popular crowd, so not being accepted into their circle wasn't a loss for me, but the women at home never ostracized me to the level I was dealing with here in America! They certainly didn't verbalize their thoughts either! I deduced that what they thought of me was none of my business and didn't add any value to my life, so losing any sleep over it was no use. Although I longed for female companionship to help me navigate my new normal, I didn't go out of my way to find it. That's not who I am. It needed to happen organically.

I ended up moving to a spacious house in a better neighborhood. A family was living next door, and I thought it was a single father with three kids. I hadn't seen signs of a mom for a long time, so I thought the guy was doing it all. One day, there was a knock on my door, so I went to see who it was. In my culture, you don't just show up at anyone's house unless you've established a relationship with them. So, in my mind, I answered in my dialect, "WHO YOU IS?" In reality, I quietly peered through the peephole, and all I saw were glasses! I don't open my door to anyone as a standard rule, so I stood there looking at her while she was knocking. It was only after she backed up to leave and I could see her entire face that I spoke. She introduced herself to me as the neighbor from next door, wanting to welcome me and my family to the neighborhood. I thought, "Who does that?" She seemed friendly enough, so I let her in.

I told her my thoughts, thinking the guy who lived next door was a single father, and we both laughed. She had such a pleasant smile, a realness in her eyes, and an easy conversation that let me know I could trust her. We found out we were both married to men who served in the armed forces, and we both had three kids. She had two boys and a girl, and I had two girls and a boy. What were the odds? Also, she worked the third shift, so that's why I never saw her. She slept while we were at work, and she worked while we slept! Mystery solved! We learned a lot from that conversation and became fast friends. Over the years, our kids or husbands would fight, but our relationship remained solid. We lived so close that we would hear each other's arguments with our spouses and children, so of course, we had to address the elephants in the room when we got together. We confided in each other about the good, bad, and ugly aspects of our lives and gave each other the support and advice we both longed for. Simultaneously, I connected with other women like her who would gain my trust and friendship, but my circle is still small. With over twenty years of friendship, they are still a part of my tribe!

Why am I so cautious of whom I let into my tribe? Not everyone who says they're your friend *is* your friend! I'm a girl's girl, and I believe that picking the right women for your tribe is essential for personal growth and well-being. I'm a big energy person, and I believe in the law of attraction. Your vibe determines your tribe! I give off positive vibes only because I have found that having a group of supportive and like-minded friends can have a profound impact on my life. As an Afro-Caribbean woman, my tribe has helped me get more acclimated to the African American experience. As I didn't grow up with racism, I needed to understand what that meant for me and my family living in America, and they were the best teachers of that. I had to be a different, tougher woman if I were to also face racism and teach my children how to be strong in the face of it. The women in my tribe have been there for me during my toughest times, offering me a shoulder to cry on and a listening ear. They have also celebrated my successes with me and pushed me to become the best version of myself, and I provided all of that for them as well. We've been through marriages, divorces, births, deaths, job woes, you name it! We ride hard for each other and make time to laugh and enjoy each other. That's what it's all about! Having the right women in my tribe means I am surrounded by a positive and uplifting community that encourages me to reach my goals, tap into my power, and walk in my purpose.

Another reason why picking the right women for your tribe is important is that it helps build meaningful relationships. Like the women in my tribe, the women you choose should share your values and interests, which helps you to have a deep connection that goes beyond surface-level interactions. Having a strong community of intelligent, loyal, and fabulous women in my life has given me a sense of belonging and helped me feel less alone in the world. You should aspire to that for yourself.

Picking the right women for my tribe was important because it also helped me to cultivate a positive mindset of love and light. These women are optimistic and have a growth mindset, which inspires me to approach life in the same way. They encourage me to see challenges as opportunities for growth and to focus on the positive aspects of my life. Being around such positive and supportive women helps me to maintain a positive outlook on life, even during difficult times. This experience has thoroughly outweighed the experiences I had when I first moved to Illinois, and I'm grateful for them. I take friendship very seriously, so if I call you my friend, that means I hold you in very high regard. I don't trust easily. Trust is earned, and once you've earned mine, you have a sis for life. Be yourself and let your friendships come organically. You should also be just as selective and careful of whom you align yourself with as I am.

Now, let's talk about what to look for when building your tribe, because vibes don't lie, but sometimes, people do. As you're being intentional about your circle, pay attention to the green flags: women who celebrate your wins like they're their own, those who hold you accountable with love and grace, who listen to understand instead of just waiting to talk. Look for consistency: the ones who show up, not only when it's convenient, and whose energy lifts your spirit instead of draining it. On the flip side, those red flags can bring negative energy to your life, so don't ignore them. Be mindful of those sisters who always have a slick remark when you're doing well, who gossip more than they grow, or only pop up when they need something. Watch out for those who push your boundaries, dismiss your feelings, or leave you feeling empty instead of empowered. Choosing your tribe is sacred work. This is your inner circle, which will either help you grow or keep you stuck. So, take your time, trust your gut, and don't hand out seats at your table just because of history or habit. You're building something beautiful, and it deserves to be protected. Period! As you start your journey of building your tribe, "Beware of the company you keep!"

What standards are required to be invited into your tribe?

_____

_____

_____

_____

_____

_____

_____

_____

_____

_____

_____

_____

_____

_____

_____

_____

_____

How will you know if someone can contribute to your tribe?

"*Be a woman other women can trust. Have the courage to tell another woman directly when she has offended, hurt, or disappointed you. Successful women have a loyal tribe of loyal and honest women behind them. Not haters. Not backstabbers or women who whisper behind their back. Be a woman who lifts other women.*"

~ Sophia A. Nelson

What Happens In The Tribe...
Stays In The Tribe

*H*ave you ever had a friend who always tells you everyone's business but will look you straight in the eyes and say, "Don't tell anyone what I just told you?" I do! This is the type of person who will sit and "pung melee" or gossip all day! It's all well and good until your business is told. We have a saying in the Virgin Islands, "Who bring come...carry!" It means, "A person who will bring/tell you someone else's business will also carry/tell your business to someone else!" Now, what is the lesson to be learned here? You guessed it...you can't trust this person. You may be able to talk about surface-level things like what happens at work, the weather, and maybe the kids. You definitely will have to refrain from telling them anything about your relationship or anything else in your personal life because they can't hold water!

My mother was notorious for this behavior. My mom never left the house, but she knew everyone's business, and she was not afraid to tell it! Sometimes, it was funny the things she said until a sibling shared something she told them about me. Then it was a problem! Living on an island has its perks and its drawbacks! It's great to visit and make great memories on your vacation. However, living there is another story. The island is only thirty-two square miles long, so everyone knows everyone. The minute something happens, it spreads around the island like wildfire! You can almost expect to have your business in the streets, whether it's true or not. In a sisterhood, you don't want someone who will tell your business! There must be an unspoken rule of trust and loyalty. Your tribe is an extension of yourself. Now, granted, people aren't going to treat you the same way you treat them, but you at least want the basic aspects of loyalty, right?

Trust and loyalty are crucial components of any strong relationship, and this is especially true in sisterhood. When you have a sister, you have a lifelong companion who will be there for you through thick and thin. Trust is the foundation of this bond, and it is essential to establish it early on. Just like in a romantic relationship, you want to see if the person is aligned with your standards and views on friendship, and you can't overlook the red flags. Trust enables us as sisters to confide in one another, whether we're spilling tea, sharing our fears and hopes, or offering support in times of need. We also want to ensure that the people we're sharing with will keep our secrets between us and not spill them to the sister circle or anyone else behind our backs. "What happens in Vegas…stays in Vegas!" The same rules apply to our sisterhood. Without trust, how can we be vulnerable with one another? That means the bond between us will suffer.

Loyalty is also an essential part of sisterhood. It means standing by your sister no matter what, being there for her when she needs you, and having her back when she faces challenges. Loyalty means being a constant source of support, even when things get tough. In sisterhood, loyalty is a two-way street, and it's important that both parties feel it and honor it. When you know your sister has your back, you can tackle anything life throws your way. For me, it means you also have my back when I'm not there. I've had a couple of situations where others told my friends something about me that wasn't true, and my friends believed it without giving me the benefit of the doubt! Why? Here's why that hurt me. I expect my friends to know my character, so when these situations arise, they can defend me and say, "That doesn't sound like my friend. Let me talk with her." When that doesn't happen, it makes me reconsider the loyalty of our friendship. It calls every conversation we've had to the carpet and leaves me with questions like,

"Are you really my friend? What do you *really* think of me?"

Sisterhood isn't just about the good times; it's about how we navigate the tough times, too. Disagreements are inevitable, but how we handle them determines whether we strengthen or strain our bond. Instead of letting a misunderstanding fester, address it with love and honesty. "Hey, friend, it didn't sit right with me when you said that. Can we talk about it?" Starting a conversation this way keeps the focus on resolution rather than blame. On the flip side, if a sister approaches you about an issue, listen with an open heart instead of getting defensive. "I hear you, and that wasn't my intention. I appreciate you telling me, and I'll be more mindful moving forward." This kind of response defuses tension and shows that you value the relationship more than being right.

But what if trust has already been broken? Rebuilding trust takes time, consistency, and accountability. If you've hurt your girlfriend, own up to it and make amends. A genuine apology sounds like: "I realize I hurt you, and I take full responsibility. That was never my intention, but I understand how it affected you. I value our friendship, and I want to do better." Done and dusted! From then on, what you do will matter more than what you say. Show up, be reliable, and give the relationship time to heal.

Okay, now let's be real. Sometimes, the apology never comes. Not everyone is willing to take accountability, and waiting for an apology that may never come will only drain your spirit, girl. In those cases, you must decide: Is this relationship worth salvaging, or is it time to move forward without resentment?

If the bond is worth keeping, focus on how the person shows up moving forward. Some people express remorse through actions rather than words. But if trust feels beyond repair, you can release the hurt without carrying bitterness or at least take steps toward it. Forgiveness doesn't mean allowing the same hurt again, it means freeing yourself from it. True sisterhood isn't about never making mistakes. It's about being willing to repair, learn, and grow. Sometimes, it's about knowing when to let go with grace.

Trust and loyalty are critical in sisterhood because they create a safe space for us to just be ourselves. They are the building blocks of sisterhood and are essential to maintaining a strong and sustainable bond. When we can trust one another and are loyal to each other, we feel free to express ourselves honestly and authentically without fear of judgment. We can share our deepest secrets, dreams, and fears without hesitation. This openness and vulnerability can help us form an even deeper bond, becoming a lifelong source of strength, love, and the kind of connection that makes you a girl's girl.

But even the strongest bonds will be tested, and how we handle conflict matters. Resolving issues with honesty and care helps protect the foundation of sisterhood. However, when trust is broken beyond repair, moving forward, sometimes without the apology we deserve, becomes a necessary act of self-preservation. Letting go of resentment doesn't mean forgetting; it means choosing peace over bitterness so we can continue to grow, with or without those who once held a place in our tribe.

Even after the dust settles, trust doesn't have to be a closed door; it can be cracked open again if both hearts are willing to do the work. It requires effort, time, and a whole lot of humility from both sides. When someone truly values the bond, they'll show it through consistent actions, accountability, and a willingness to listen without getting defensive. And sis, if you're the one who broke the trust, just own it. What we're not going to do is sweep it under the rug or try to spiritually bypass your way out of it by saying, "Everything happens for a reason," or "I've prayed about it, so it's all love," to dodge responsibility. Apologize sincerely, acknowledge the hurt, and give the other person space to process, because healing doesn't run on your timeline. It may need to happen over dinner and drinks or brunch, but get it done! No one should have to move on without an apology if the friendship is truly valuable to you. It's about more than just saying "sorry";

it's about reflecting on how your lack of ownership might make someone you care about feel unseen, dismissed, or disposable. Trust can be restored, and these hard conversations are also an opportunity to rebuild the foundation of the friendship—one that's stronger, more honest, and more aligned with the sisterhood you both deserve. Even if the relationship looks different afterward, different doesn't mean broken; it can mean wiser, stronger, and rooted in something real.

What can women do to strengthen trust and loyalty within our sisterhood?

_____

_____

_____

_____

_____

_____

_____

_____

_____

_____

_____

_____

_____

_____

_____

_____

_____

How do you move on without an apology from your good girlfriend?

"*Mothers view their daughters as younger versions of themselves. They look forward to all the things they can teach them, but teaching them how to form true relationships with other women is one of the most important lessons.*"

~*Norine Fahie*

Passing Down The Legacy Of Sisterhood

My mother and I had the strangest relationship. It has changed over the years, but I wish it were different. I felt so estranged from her because she has said and done some hurtful things in the past that she refused to give a genuine apology for. For us to maintain a decent relationship, I had to put those things aside so I could see her as a human being…a woman. I thought that no matter what, a mother and daughter would live this perfect life where they got along and always loved to be around each other. At least that's what it looked like on *The Cosby Show*. However, that's not how life works! It takes just the same amount of time and energy to build that bond as it does with any other relationship.

I used to say my mom never taught me anything, but when I look back on my life, she has taught me a lot.

However, when I think back on our conversations, I just wasn't listening with a woman's ear as opposed to a child's ear. The wisdom came to me when I shifted my mindset to act in my womanhood, not my childhood. Once I did that, I began looking at my world differently and applied the knowledge where I needed to. Sometimes, we don't look at our mothers as women, just as mothers. This is how I missed the value of her words before. Those nuggets gave me the strength, sass, and courage to become the strong woman I am today!

I thought Mom was the best cook in the world. She taught me to cook my first meal, which was scrambled eggs. Then I moved my way up to macaroni and cheese, and as I got older, we added more things like baking. Her baking rivaled that of Martha Stewart. I loved helping her bake around the holidays. It was the best time of year to learn because there was so much that needed to be baked. She always needed a sous chef, and I was always a willing participant. Not because I got to lick the spoon or the bowl, but because she taught me how to do everything from grating coconut or carrots to how much spice to add, and how to test to see if the food was done. The best part, besides tasting everything, of course, was all the hot tea she would spill, telling everyone's business, and sharing how their cakes weren't as delicious as hers because of what she does differently! I realized Mom was a little competitive...and funny!

On the other end of the spectrum, seeing Mom interacting with other women was insightful and hilarious. Mom and my auntie were super close, and they would call each other so often that sometimes, as I took Mom the phone, I thought, "Lawd…wah Auntie want again! She just speak to Mommy. Dem does pung deh most melee mehson!" YES, my thoughts are in my dialect! Mommy and Auntie were the Melee Queens in my eyes. They knew everyone's business, but they also loved sharing with each other. Island people were already loud, but when those two got together, chile, put cotton in your ears! I just loved the ease of conversation and the respect and love they had for each other. This was my favorite auntie, whom I was named after, so I didn't mind being around or talking to her.

Auntie lived in the British Virgin Islands, so when she came to visit, this was when the magic happened. There were always great conversations and plenty of eating going on. I grew up knowing that children were to be seen and not heard, so I played into this because I wanted to hang around to hear all the juicy gossip! So, of course, I'm the little helper bringing glasses of water, juice, and whatever food or baked goods would keep my nosey behind in earshot of these conversations. Auntie had such a positive spirit. She gave us the best hugs and always greeted us with a smile that let us know everything would be ok. I saw a different side of my mother when Auntie dropped in. She seemed easy, laughing, making jokes, just being herself… very connected to her source…free. She also displayed this persona with other women, but not like with Auntie. Mom and the other women in their circle were loyal to each other and had a great bond. Some of her friends were career women, and my mother was a domestic engineer. Yep…she stayed home with more than four kids on any given day. There were nine of us, so whoever wasn't in school was at home. I'm sure those visits must have been lifelines for her, keeping her afloat in ways we could never understand.

Watching these relationships was amazing. There were times when they seemed to talk in code because the house was small, and of course, we were listening. Often, one said only a word or two, and they all nodded in agreement or laughed out loud. They all talked at once and ended sentences at the same time, and sometimes they just sat and visited quietly. I didn't really get it, but I knew that I liked it. I got it once I was old enough and had formed my friendships. That's what sisterhood looked like. I understood the importance of conversation among women who really knew, accepted, and showed great respect toward each other. They have grown and bonded together through life's hard lessons and unexpected detours. They never had a need or patience for any pretense. They were a tribe…my first real example of sisterhood.

The lessons I learned by watching Mom and her circle were invaluable to me. However, it would've been nice to be invited to the discussions to get firsthand experience instead of being on the outside looking in. Nevertheless, that was a different time, and I certainly had to stay in a child's place.

I do feel it's essential for mothers to teach their daughters about sisterhood as it helps to foster a sense of community, belonging, and support among women. By nurturing this bond, mothers can teach their daughters how to uplift, empower, and advocate for each other. They can encourage their daughters to build meaningful relationships with other young ladies and older women, which can help to strengthen their emotional well-being and social skills.

As mothers, we can instill the values of sisterhood in our daughters by modeling it ourselves. By treating other women with respect, kindness, and compassion, we can show our daughters the importance of building positive relationships with others. We can also encourage our daughters to participate in activities that promote sisterhood, such as sports teams, clubs, sororities, or volunteer organizations. I used to take my daughters with me to most of my women's business meetings when they were younger. I even had them dress in business attire and involved them in some of the discussions. I wanted them to experience in person how the dynamics were between women. Now that they're women, I still involve them in my women's community groups.

Teaching our daughters about sisterhood also helps to challenge gender stereotypes and inequality. By promoting the idea that women can uplift and support each other, we can help our daughters develop a more positive self-image and challenge societal norms that often pit women against each other or give them the perception that other women are competition. Finally, we can also teach our daughters about empathy and how to listen and respond to the needs of others. By doing so, we can help them become better communicators and problem-solvers, which will serve them well throughout their lives as they form their tribes.

But let's be real, passing down the legacy of sisterhood isn't just for the mamas. If you don't have daughters, that doesn't mean your impact stops there. This kind of love and wisdom is too powerful to keep to yourself. You've got nieces, goddaughters, mentees, bonus daughters, even young women you work with every day, looking at how you move. They're paying attention. So, whether you're sharing lessons over lunch, dropping gems in a meeting, or just being that safe space someone needs, you're still planting seeds. That's a legacy, too. It's not about titles or blood; it's about being intentional with your influence. When you live what you preach, you're showing the next woman what sisterhood really looks like. And trust me, the way you show up might inspire someone in ways you'll never know.

> *What have you been taught about sisterhood, and have you shared what you've learned with the girls and women in your circle?*

_____

_____

_____

_____

_____

_____

_____

_____

_____

_____

_____

_____

_____

_____

_____

_____

_____

_____

What are some ways you can encourage and assist them in building their tribe?

_____

_____

_____

_____

_____

_____

_____

_____

_____

_____

_____

_____

_____

_____

_____

The success of every woman should be the inspiration to another. We should raise each other up. Make sure you're very courageous: be strong, be extremely kind, and above all be humble."

~Serena Williams

Why Do Some Women Always Side-Eye Others?

*I*f you know me personally, you will know I'm a girl's girl. I appreciate and value myself as a woman, and I appreciate and value other women. I have no issues co-existing with other women because I see them as my equals. Unfortunately, that is not the case for everyone. Some women feel the need to compete with others, and I just don't get it! What is the purpose of this? I had an incident where I worked with a young lady who I thought was very nice. We became friends to the point that she felt comfortable telling me about the private details of her marriage. I was there to listen and not judge, and I was very careful to be sensitive and honest with the advice I gave…solicited, of course! There was trust between us, and I shared about my pending divorce as well, but I was a bit more cautious because I was still vetting her. A job opening came up, and we both applied, unbeknownst to either of us. After a while, we both realized the coincidence and wished each other well on our journey. We made a pact that our relationship would not change, no matter who got the job. As it turns out, I got the job, and she didn't hold up her end of the bargain. Suddenly, she didn't want to speak with me and always made an excuse not to be available as she was before, even though I knew she wasn't that busy with her job. I didn't question her and attributed her behavior to the issues she was having in her marriage.

Everything came to a head when the most bizarre thing happened. Walking down the hallway heading for the bathroom, I saw her speaking with someone in a cubicle. Feeling a bit uneasy about the shift in our friendship, I looked away to gather my thoughts when I saw her. I was going to say hi and ask if she was ok. She didn't know I saw her, but the moment she saw me, she ducked into the cubicle to avoid me, and the lady she was speaking with gave me the glare of death! That hurt my feelings because I had no idea what warranted either of their behavior! I shared what happened with another friend in our workgroup, and that's when I got the real tea. Evidently, she was upset that I got the job, and she didn't! Now, what did that have to do with me? I rocked my interview and pitched myself in such a way that I impressed the hiring managers. Not to mention, I have a great personality!

Okuur!

What she did was unnecessary. Apparently, I was in a one-sided competition! Why? Only God would know. Why do some women always side-eye others? Why is there a need to compete with other women? In society, do we not have similar struggles? I say similar because the black woman's struggle in America is real, and not all women understand the strength we must harness to make it through our day! I would never compete with other women. I see them as my equals.

We have historically been competitively pitted against each other. This kind of behavior often leads to jealousy, resentment, and even backstabbing. We need to recognize that competing is not necessary and is counterproductive.

One of the main reasons we don't need to compete is that there is already enough societal pressure and competition placed on us. Let's start with how the media often perpetuates unrealistic beauty standards. Not to mention how we're often pitted against each other in the workplace and other areas of life. When we compete, it only reinforces these negative messages and can create a very toxic environment. Don't we have enough to worry about running successful businesses, being great mothers, daughters, mentors, and friends, and being ladies in the streets and freaks in the sheets? That's a lot! We don't need anything else to drive a wedge between us when we can learn so much from each other.

Working as a unit allows us to pool our resources, experiences, knowledge, and skills. It creates a sense of community and fosters a supportive environment where women can help each other grow and succeed. When women come together and work toward a common goal, we can achieve so many amazing things. This type of collaboration can lead to innovation, creativity, and positive change.

When we work together, the world can't help but notice. It shows that we can achieve great things when we support each other and work together. This kind of unity can break down stereotypes and inspire other women to join the cause. It can inspire a movement, encouraging other women to work together in their communities and spheres of influence.

Another avenue we need to consider is that sisterhood looks different across cultures. How women connect, communicate, and even express affection can vary based on our origin stories. As a proud Caribbean woman, I've seen firsthand how cultural norms and values influence how we view and treat each other.

In Caribbean culture, sisterhood is often a blend of fierce loyalty and tough love. We'll defend you to the end but call you out when you're wrong, sometimes bluntly. You gotta have thick skin, girlie! If a Caribbean sister sees you slipping, she'll check you, no sugarcoating. It might feel harsh, but it comes from a place of love. However, to someone from a culture that values more subtle communication, it may be too abrasive. This cultural difference can sometimes create misunderstandings. I know first-hand what that's like! What one woman perceives as "just keeping it real," another might take as judgment or shade.

Upbringing and traditions also play a crucial role. In many Caribbean families, women are raised to be strong and resilient, sometimes to a fault. We are taught to push through struggles with a "suck it up" mentality. This cultural strength can make vulnerability feel uncomfortable or even weak. As a result, we might side-eye women who are more openly emotional, misinterpreting their softness as weakness, when in reality, their openness is a form of strength. But this is why we must all come to the table and have open discussions. Cultural diversity needs to be acknowledged and embraced if we are to achieve mutual understanding.

Communication styles also differ across cultures. Caribbean women tend to be more direct and outspoken, while women from other cultures may prioritize politeness or subtlety. For example, a Caribbean sister might say,

"Gyal, wah yuh deh pon—stop lollygaggin' and make it happen!" While someone from a culture that values gentler language may say, "Hey sis, I've noticed you've been struggling a bit. Do you want to talk?" Without understanding the cultural lens, we can misread each other's intentions.

From my experience, I put my foot in my mouth while talking to a friend who couldn't make it to my birthday party by saying, "One monkey don't stop no show!" Oh, I definitely got the side-eye! The translation meant, "Although you aren't going to make it, we'll miss you, but we'll still carry on." I was unaware that the word "monkey" was a derogatory term for African American people, as I didn't grow up with racism. I was quickly schooled, apologized profusely, and committed that foot-in-mouth moment to memory! A key lesson here is not to assume that because we share the same race, we automatically understand each other's cultural struggles.

To strengthen sisterhood across cultures, we have to practice empathy and give grace. Instead of assuming another woman is being shady, we should consider that her behavior might be shaped by her cultural norms. The next time you catch yourself side-eyeing a sister from a different background, pause and ask yourself, "Is this about her or my assumptions?" By embracing cultural diversity, we expand our capacity for compassion and connection and reduce unconscious bias.

Sis, we do not need to compete or be jealous of each other. Let's put our energy into working together as a unit, supporting each other, lifting each other, and fixing each other's crowns without letting the world know it was crooked. Let's focus on getting on a different vibration! This kind of collaboration can only lead to great things. Let's move with purpose and let the world feel the shift, especially to our little sisters watching our every move. We need to be sure the example is set, and those stiletto indentations are deep enough so they can see them and make some indentations of their own. Working together will break down stereotypes, inspire positive change, build bridges between generations and cultural differences, and create a brighter future for all women.

Let's unpack this. How do we *actually* stop competing and start collaborating? It all starts with checking ourselves. We gotta pause and ask, *"Why did that bother me?"* or *"Is this really about her… or something I need to deal with inside myself?"* That kind of self-checking takes honesty, but it's where the real growth happens.

So, here's an exercise for you: grab your journal and write about a time you felt that competitive ache toward another woman. No judgment, just be real girl. Then flip the script. Write down three things you admire about her. When you start turning comparison into inspiration, whew chile! That's a whole mindset shift.

Let me drop this in your spirit, too, sis. Practice celebrating other women, *out loud*. Not just the big wins, but the little ones too. Shoot your girl a "Yesss queen!" text, repost her business, or hype her up in the group chat. It's like a muscle, the more you work it, the easier it gets to big up your sisters without that lil' sting of envy creeping in.

And let me say this: Your circle matters. Being around women who are secure in themselves and genuinely root for each other? That energy is contagious! It helps you stay focused on your lane and not get caught up in side-eyes and silent battles.

What can we do as a sisterhood to eliminate the stigma that women need to compete?

Do you pause to consider the cultural background and unique experiences of the women around you before making assumptions about their actions or intentions?

_____

_____

_____

_____

_____

_____

_____

_____

_____

_____

_____

_____

_____

_____

_____

_____

_____

"I am not my sister's keeper. I am my sister."

~Iyanla Vanzant

Are You Your Sister's Keeper?

*H*ow far will you go to protect your friendships? Are you a ride-or-die friend? Can you tell your friends when they're wrong? Female friendships can be a lot, but if all parties know what's expected, they can be very fulfilling. Being your sister's keeper means taking responsibility for the well-being of your sister and being there for her whenever she needs you, like offering a listening ear, helping with practical tasks and problem-solving, and being there to offer emotional support. Lord knows we all need a little of that! Knowing someone has your back unconditionally gives you such a sense of security and belonging.

Being your sister's keeper requires a deep sense of empathy and a willingness to put her needs before your own. Have you ever gone to a friend to talk about an issue, and she ends up making the entire conversation about her? How rude! That happened to me. I ended up helping her through her issues, and mine were thrown by the wayside. It was as though mine weren't interesting or important enough, or she didn't know how to ask for help and was just waiting for the opportunity to get it out. Either way, that was not very sisterly. There was plenty of opportunity to handle both issues. When your sister approaches you for help, it is best to just get out a couple of glasses of your best wine and a good charcuterie board and get comfortable. Or, in my case, a plate of rice and peas, curry goat, and plantains with a cold glass of mauby. We're getting real comfortable! It is important for her to feel heard and have some resolve at the end of the conversation, or an idea of how to solve the issue.

One of the most important aspects of being your sister's keeper is building a strong and supportive relationship. This involves spending time together, sharing experiences, and cultivating a deep understanding of each other's hopes, dreams, and fears. By doing so, you can create a sense of trust and mutual support that will allow you to be there for each other no matter what challenges you may face.

Being your sister's keeper means standing up for her and advocating for her. Whether she is facing discrimination, injustice, or other challenges, you have a responsibility to support her and help her navigate these difficult situations. This may involve speaking on her behalf, providing emotional support, or helping her find resources and support to overcome these challenges.

Ultimately, being your sister's keeper is about creating a deep and lasting bond that will help both of you thrive. By supporting each other through life's ups and downs, you can build a relationship that will last a lifetime and help each other become the best versions of yourselves. Whether you are siblings by birth or by choice, being your sister's keeper is a powerful and meaningful commitment that can enrich your lives in countless ways.

Being your sister's keeper isn't all rainbows and sunshine, though! Being a great friend also entails telling your girl when she's wrong! Sorry, sis…you're not always right, and you need to come to terms with that! How else can we grow into the women God intended us to be if we move through life thinking we're always right and no one can tell us otherwise? What kind of friend would I be if I said nothing? Well, if you're my friend, I'm sure enough sitting you down to give you piping hot tea on how you were wrong. Don't worry, though, I will build you up in the end!

Telling your sister when she's wrong is an essential aspect of building a strong and healthy relationship. While it may be tempting to avoid confrontation or spare her feelings, honesty and constructive feedback play a crucial role in personal growth and development. By pointing out her mistakes or misguided actions, you are not only helping her recognize her errors but also encouraging her to learn from them. Open communication fosters trust and allows for meaningful conversations where she can reflect on her choices and make better decisions in the future. It demonstrates that you care enough about her well-being to provide honest feedback, even if it may be uncomfortable at the moment. Be sure you bring your sister-to-English translation book with you, though. It is imperative to not only say what you have to say but also remember who you're speaking with so you can point these things out respectfully. Even if she's out in these streets wildin', chile, try your best not to be judgy and condescending. When you speak in a tone of love, she will be able to hear you and understand your point of view and instruction. We still love her. We just want to let her know her behavior might be a bit ratchet, which is concerning.

However, it is equally important to balance your feedback by building your sister up after addressing her mistakes. Constructive criticism should always be accompanied by encouragement, support, and reassurance. Offering words of affirmation and highlighting her strengths and achievements can help soften the impact of the critique and maintain a positive atmosphere. By focusing on her potential and reminding her of her capabilities, you instill confidence and motivate her to persist in her endeavors. This combination of honesty and encouragement not only strengthens your bond as sisters but also empowers her to learn from her mistakes, grow as an individual, and strive for excellence. She may not be happy with you for a little bit, but that's the drawback of being a good sister! She'll be a'ight!

Ladies, let's get into it. We all know there's a difference between having your friend's back and turning a blind eye when she's moving sideways. Support doesn't mean co-signing behavior that's toxic, self-destructive, or harmful to others. Being your sister's keeper means loving her enough to say, "Nah, girl, that ain't it," even when it's uncomfortable. It's knowing when to extend grace and when to set boundaries. Sometimes, love shows up as tough conversations, not just cheerleading. As for me, if I can't cover you and correct you, then we have to reevaluate the friendship. As your sis, I will never let you fall. I'm there for you, girlie!

In these sister relationships, we can't mistake loyalty for enabling. If we genuinely care about someone, we need to be brave enough to hold up the mirror when needed and help them course-correct with love. That's real sisterhood, walking alongside each other in truth, not just comfort.

When we do that, we don't just protect the friendship; we protect her growth. And trust, when the dust settles, she'll thank you for not letting her settle for less than her best.

How can I effectively balance the responsibility of being my sister's keeper while allowing her the freedom to make her own choices and learn from her own experiences?

In what ways can I support my sister's emotional well-being and provide a safe space for her to share her struggles and vulnerabilities, as her keeper?

_____

_____

_____

_____

_____

_____

_____

_____

_____

_____

_____

_____

_____

_____

_____

_____

_____

"*Having a blood sister is like having a built-in best friend. We share a history, a bond, and a love that is unbreakable. Through thick and thin, we stand together, supporting and uplifting each other. Our sisterhood is a source of strength, resilience, and empowerment.*"

~*Unknown*

Bound By Blood

*W*hen you grow up with sisters, it's not only loud, but it is also a bit crowded, especially if you all share one room. Not to mention all the different personalities you had to work with daily! Sometimes, it was funny to see the personalities clash, but that can get old quickly. Growing up in the vibrant backdrop of the Caribbean was a unique experience that shaped our bond in extraordinary ways. Our strict parents, driven by their protective and conservative nature, never allowed us the freedom to venture outside and play like the other kids in the neighborhood. While this might have initially felt limiting, it ultimately forged an unbreakable connection between us siblings. Our shared circumstances became the canvas upon which we painted our world of imagination and creativity.

I'm aging myself, but I remember playing Chinese jump rope, not this new version they're doing now. The old-school version. We also played with jacks and marbles and played red-light-green-light. The highlight for me was skating across the floors. So, Dad redid the floors with ceramic tiles, so it was nice and shiny, but most importantly… smooth. Perfect for skating. When they left instructions for the floors to be mopped, it was on! We got soapy water and soaked the entire kitchen, living room, and hallway floors. Then, one by one, we did a little run and then got down on our knees and skated like seasoned ice skaters…unbeknownst to my parents, of course. Can't do that now, though. These knees *will* protest! This was all to give ourselves some semblance of happiness because summers sucked! When school was out in the summer, my dad instructed the older siblings to have school with us. Boring! Who wants to have school when we're officially out of school? Chile…my parents! We had no life, so we grew up sheltered and had to get really creative to entertain ourselves.

As we became adults, we grew into our own. We all got married and had children. Not all at once, but our kids are close in age. Over the years, there have been highs and lows in our relationships. There have been petty arguments and funny moments, but despite living in different areas, we tried our best to keep our sisterhood afloat. My sisters all have different personalities, and they definitely live up to them.

The mom of the group always gave unsolicited advice. She thought she knew it all. Most times, she was a plethora of information, but other times, she was just telling everyone what to do. In her role, she gained our respect because she was smart and just knew what to do in most situations. Yet, behind her composed exterior lies the weight of her self-imposed duties, at times burdening her with a responsibility that felt overwhelming. Despite the burden, she continued to guide us with firm dedication, though secretly craving moments of reprieve from the expectations placed upon her capable shoulders. At times, she forgot she was our sister and not a parent. She was tough but always made time to provide some good sister wisdom and sometimes some juicy gossip.

The drama queen is just that…drama! She means well, but she can't help herself. She is highly intelligent and can talk from dawn to dusk. There's never a dull moment. Sometimes, the conversations were about parenting, religion, current events, and relationships. Every interaction with her is akin to stepping onto a stage where she is the star, and the world is merely her audience. She would draw you in with her stories, and before you knew it, two hours had passed. She governs with an innate affinity for theatrics, commanding attention effortlessly, yet her heart tells a longing for validation and acceptance. Though she offers her time generously, her attention darts like a butterfly, always returning to the center of her universe–herself. Despite the layers of ego and vanity, a tender vulnerability peeks through, like a delicate bloom amid thorns, reminding us that beneath the self-centered exterior lies a sister longing to be understood and loved.

Next is the free spirit, who is unlike anyone you would ever meet. Like a chameleon, she could morph into any character at a moment's notice. She was the Jane of all trades and master of all. Within the fabric of our family's story, my sister emerges as a vivid thread, weaving her way through life's intricacies with an insatiable thirst for adventure and knowledge, which still gets her into trouble sometimes. Everywhere she goes, she leaves a trail of captivated minds in her wake, drawn to her magnetic charisma and vast curiosity. Despite her hunger for attention, her heart remains incessantly generous and fiercely loyal to those she loves. Her journey has been marked by adversity, but like a phoenix rising from the ashes, she emerged, utilizing her past struggles as stepping stones to elevate herself to greater heights. Each obstacle she faced became a testament to her resilience, shaping her into the formidable force she is today. Deep within her soul, she wants social validation instead of validating herself. She uses her desire to seek attention as a shield, deflecting attention from the vulnerabilities she guards so fiercely.

Picture the social butterfly, all about the glitz and glam, but she can be a handful. She's used to getting her own way and can be pretty blunt, which can sting sometimes. She can read you for filth in the same tone of voice as she would use to ask you to pass the milk! But don't underestimate her; she's street-smart and knows how to handle herself. Deep down, though, she feels a bit like she doesn't quite fit in and wishes she got the same respect as everyone else. She's all about fairness and expects others to treat her as well as she treats them, and she deserves that. And when you earn her love, she'll stick by you through thick and thin.

As for myself, I'm like the backbone of our family – the sister who keeps everything running smoothly. Lots of people see me as the glue that holds us all together, the one they come to when they need help or advice. I'm good at looking out for everyone, and I'm always there when someone needs support. But not everyone thinks I'm as important as others do. Some wonder if relying on me so much is really a good thing or if it just makes everyone too dependent on me. Despite what people say, I'm determined to keep our family close-knit, even if not everyone agrees with how I do it.

Although we're all different, one thing connects us. We are all lovers of love. Currently, some of my sisters and

I are estranged for one reason or another. We all fight just as hard as we love, and if we didn't care, we wouldn't fight at all. I'm a Gemini spirit, so I don't hold grudges. It is a complete waste of energy and time. Time that would be best suited to mend our sisterhood. My relationship with my sisters is more important to me than holding a grudge or allowing my pride and ego to take over. Life is so short, and we have to be cognizant of how we utilize the time we have left. I would rather spend the rest of my life trying to unite my blood sisterhood than watching everyone have petty arguments with each other. We may not say it out loud, but in the depths of our hearts, we have a genuine love for the person we're not speaking with. Some of them just haven't learned how to let go and move on without an apology, or they would rather stop speaking to you without even telling you what's wrong. Either way, I love them all and I'm here to be a listening ear, a shoulder to cry on, or give a knee apology. Whatever it takes.

Family is important to me. They're the ones you should be able to celebrate with when things are going well and seek solace when things are bad. Although my family is not as close as we used to be, at least some of us speak to each other. Hey, that's life, right? A win is a win. One day, we may be able to take that sister's trip…fingers crossed! Still, even with the change in dynamics, I hope our bond will reignite because sisterhood, in any form, is worth nurturing.

Sisterhood runs deeper than words; it's a bond built on shared history, childhood memories, and an unspoken understanding of where you come from. But life has a way of pulling sisters in different directions. Misunderstandings, distance, or even old wounds can create gaps that feel too wide to cross. The truth is, sisterhood isn't about being perfect; it's about being present. Even the smallest effort of sending a quick text, sharing a laugh over an old memory, or choosing to let go of past hurts can make all the difference. Staying connected, even in small ways, keeps that bond alive.

When you take the step to rekindle your relationship with your sister, you're creating space for healing, growth, and support. Time moves fast, and waiting for the "perfect moment" to reach out might mean missing the opportunity altogether. No one understands your journey quite like your sister does, and even if you see things differently, that doesn't mean you can't find common ground. It's not about agreeing on everything; it's about valuing your relationship enough to stay in each other's lives. Knowing you have someone who shares your roots and your story brings a sense of belonging that nothing else can replace.

At the end of the day, reconnecting isn't just about revisiting the past; it's about building a future together. Your sister is one of the few people who truly knows your beginning, and that bond is worth holding on to. Even if your relationship looks different than it once did, a simple check-in, a heartfelt conversation, or an occasional get-to-gether can keep your connection strong. Life will always bring challenges, but having a sister to walk with you through them is one of the greatest gifts you'll ever have.

Whether you were raised in the same household or found your way back to one another after years apart, the journey with a biological sister is full of joy and complexity. Every laugh, every disagreement you worked through, and every big or small moment you've shared help to shape the story of your relationship. If you find yourself estranged, let this be a reminder: Reconciliation doesn't require perfection; it just takes intention. A phone call, a birthday text, or even a simple "Sissy, you've been in my spirit" can reopen the door to healing.

Sisterhood by blood is not always easy, chile, I know that firsthand, but it is sacred. Cherish it. Nurture it. And when life gets busy, remember that showing up, even in small ways, can mean everything. I lost one of my sisters, and it reminded me in the most painful way that time waits for no one. Don't let pride, distance, or busyness keep you from reaching out. Because in the grand story of your life, your sister holds a chapter no one else can write.

How can sisters support each other through active listening and constructive advice?

_____

_____

_____

_____

_____

_____

_____

_____

_____

_____

_____

_____

_____

_____

_____

_____

_____

_____

The Bonds Of Sisterhood

How can sisters collaborate to empower and uplift each other's aspirations and successes?

The Bonds Of Sisterhood

"The future of sisterhood lies in the unity of shared experiences, mutual support, and respect. It is rooted in inclusivity, diversity, and the recognition of intersectional identities, fostering a culture of collaboration over competition. Women will stand in solidarity to dismantle systems of oppression and pave the way for a more equitable world for future generations."

~Norine Fahie

Redefining Sisterhood: Tomorrow's Promise

Sisterhood has always been a safe space for shared strength, truth-telling, and healing among women. Throughout this book, we've explored its many dimensions: the ties of biological sisterhood, the bonds we build with friends who become family, and the beautiful, sometimes messy, process of showing up for one another in life's highs and lows.

We've seen how sisterhood can thrive through open communication, mutual support, forgiveness, and intentional community. We've discussed rebuilding trust, honoring our differences, and creating spaces where women can be their whole selves...unapologetically. These lessons aren't just for today; they're blueprints for tomorrow.

As we look to the future, we must ask ourselves: What does modern sisterhood look like? It looks like mentoring the next woman instead of competing with her. It looks like creating room at the table for voices that have been overlooked or silenced. It looks like calling out harmful behavior *and* calling one another back into growth and accountability. It looks like showing up, when it's easy and especially when it's not.

The truth is that sisterhood is evolving. It's no longer limited to shared DNA or even shared experiences. It's about shared values: authenticity, inclusion, empathy, and empowerment. It's about making space for women from every walk of life and meeting each other with grace instead of judgment. It's about choosing collaboration over comparison.

We are the blueprint, and we have to remember that! The way we move now shapes what the next generation of women and girls will believe is possible in their relationships with one another. And that next generation? They're already here, our little sisters, the Millennials and Gen Z women who are bold, brilliant, and unafraid to challenge the norms. They're watching us. They're learning how we support or tear each other down. It's up to us to show them what it truly means to rise together.

So yes, we must be our sister's keeper, but we must also *be* our sister, holding space, showing grace, and standing in solidarity. Both can coexist beautifully. Our choices today, how we forgive, uplift, and unite, will echo for generations. Let's continue to build a culture of women who celebrate one another loudly, speak truth to power boldly, and link arms instead of turning backs and giving side-eyes.

So, here's to tomorrow's promise: a sisterhood that's inclusive, resilient, and unshakable. A sisterhood that doesn't just survive but leads, heals, and transforms. Let us S.H.A.R.E.: Strive Higher and Reclaim Empowerment. And let us pass that power on, knowing the crown we wear may be heavy, but it must be straightened and passed on gracefully and proudly, unapologetically, lighting the way for the next woman, and the next.

In what ways can you actively contribute to creating a version of sisterhood that breaks generational patterns and builds a stronger, more united future for women coming after you?

_____

_____

_____

_____

_____

_____

_____

_____

_____

_____

_____

_____

_____

_____

_____

The Bonds Of Sisterhood

What outdated beliefs about female relationships are you willing to let go of so you can help redefine sisterhood in a new, more inclusive and empowering way?

_____

_____

_____

_____

_____

_____

_____

_____

_____

_____

_____

_____

_____

_____

_____

The Bonds Of Sisterhood

Leaving Footprints Of Power

As you close this book, take a moment to reflect on the legacy you're creating. Sisterhood doesn't end with these chapters; it lives on in how you show up, how you love, and how you support the women around you. Consider the younger women who watch your example: your daughters, mentees, little sisters, and friends. What will they learn from the way you move through life in sisterhood?

Start today by reaching out to one woman. Maybe she's walking a road you've already traveled or simply needs to hear, "I see you, girl." Speak life into her. Offer your presence. Hold space for her. Sisterhood isn't just a message; it's a movement. And you are part of the legacy that lights the path forward.

Thank you for walking this journey of sisterhood with me, allowing these words to resonate, and embracing the power of our shared stories. Together, we are rewriting what it means to stand strong, uplift, and live unapologetically. Your strength, story, and sisterhood matter...now, tomorrow, and always. Let's continue to rise, together, lining the path with our footprints, making it easier for the next generation of women to find their way.